The Birth of All Things

MARCUS AMAKER

FREE VERSE PRESS

A FREE VERSE, LLC EXPERIENCE

Also by Marcus Amaker

Books

Listening To Static (2005)
Poems For Augustine (2005)
The Soft Paper Cut (2007)
The Present Presence (2012)
The Spoken Word. Selected Poems: 2003-2013 (2013)
Mantra: An Interactive Poetry Book (2015)
Empath (2017)

Music

Big Butt (1986)
Gimme Some (1987)
Play It (1988)
Say No! (1988)
Daydreamin' (1988)
All Uv the Time (1989)
Minimalism (2005)
Dealate (2005)
Escapism (2006)
1945 (2008)
Lady Phoenix (2009)
Digital Detox (2010)
The Cassette Demos (2011)
Sunday Rain (2011)
Animation (2012)
The New Foundation *(with Quentin E. Baxter)* (2014)
The Drum Machine, Part 1 (2015)
Analogue // 1-6 (2016-7)
Telemaque. (2017)
Open (2018)
Empath *(with Quentin E. Baxter)* (2018)
Empath (Variations) (2018)
Creating Empty Space (2019)
The Birth of All Things (2019)
The Weight That Holds the Animal (2019)
Rei (2019)
Contagion (2020)
Rhythm Vaccine (2020)
Muscle Memory *(with Quentin E. Baxter)* (2020)

marcusamaker.com + tapeloop.bandcamp.com

Poetry can heal. Make air where there is shallow breath. body medicine for the heart's hiatus. poem as floatation device when there are floods of dark emotion. poetry telling us what we choose to remember: we have everything we need for remedy.

ISBN: 978-1-7346737-0-8

Library of Congress Control Number: 2020933532

Front cover image by Nick Davis
Author photo by Alice Keeney
Book design by Marcus Amaker

Printed in the United States of America.

First printing edition 2020.

Published by Free Verse Press
Free Verse, LLC
Charleston, South Carolina

freeversepress.com
marcusamaker.com

The face on the cover, illustrated by Nick Davis, is beautiful because of its dark features. Hold the image to the light to see its nuance. But also remember to cradle and appreciate the blackness. This book is about that balance. We contain light and dark, living in the same body. Look at them and love them whole.

This book is for Jordan, Rei, and Kona

Tracklist

INTERLUDE // A BRIEF SUMMARY
OF WHAT THE POET CAN DO

Side 3: Flow Own Current

Side 4: Affirm the Human

OUTRO // THE ARRIVAL

TEMPO (SELF-PORTRAIT, PART 4)

Dear friends,
allow me
to reintroduce myself.
My name is
Marcus Amaker.
I came into this world
with the heartbeat of life
in the key of life -
Stevie Wonder's album
constantly spinning
in the home
of a military family
passing through
Las Vegas.

Even as a baby,
music was the only beat
that made sense
besides the beat
of my mother and father's heart.

It was the only rhythm
that felt unforced.
Unlike my voice
that stuttered as a child,
stammered as a teen, and
still stumbles as an adult.

I beat myself up
the first time
words bumped against my breath.
My brain
disconnected from the
pulse inside my head,
So I made beats alone
behind closed doors, instead.

singing into cassette tapes
became a diary of melody.
Music became
the sibling I never had,
a best friend
for any swing of mood.
METALLICA: aggression.
JANET JACKSON: joy.
PRINCE: confidence.
JIMMY JAM AND TERRY LEWIS:
the soul of a black boy
now living in Japan.

And then I discovered
the beat of hip hop.
A TRIBE CALLED QUEST
was a journey
that left rap's permanent
impression on my tongue.
words started
forming from boom bap,
the beat of black experience.

Hip-hop was a baby
who taught me
how to speak.
I merged with its movement,
I still swing
to its beat.

With college
came the unchained melodies
of JONI MITCHELL,
TORI AMOS, ANI DIFRANCO
and PJ HARVEY.
Every night
I absorbed the beat
of women's voices
into broken-hearted poems.
In tune with
the downbeat of black wings,
spiraling through depression.

I've lived
a lifetime
of repetition and melancholy
as muscle memory
but came out stronger.

My wife knows
the ebb and flow
of my beat.

we write songs
together without
the accent of sound.

She is my melody
until the beat of time
goes silent.

Side 1

The Womb's Head-space

Mission Statement

I pledge
to not go
out of my way
for someone
who is
in the way,

to only be busy
creating empty space,

to let silence
lead me in its dance,

to welcome anxiety
at the door
but never let him
stay the night,

to have
a place to put the darkness
before the lights
turn on,

to know that,
at one point,
I wanted everything
that I have,

and to remind myself
that it's okay
when I don't
remember
these things.

A Doctor Tells Us It's Not a Life or Death Situation

Before my daughter's lungs
found a consistent rhythm,
they were off beat. Coming in

on the one, one, three, two. Unsteady
and unsettled. Too fast, and not
finishing the notes. The nurses

are worried. Concerned
with her cadence. My mother was
once scared for mine because

she found *Live Through This*
on my nightstand. It was a threat.
A kind of music she didn't

understand. A specialist comes
and gives us the notes my daughter
should be playing. He sounds like

sheet music of worry. I tell myself she
is already a fan of Ornette Coleman.
Or Autechre. Imagine that: A baby

who'll skip lullabies for bebop and
experimental electronic music. Instead,
they hook her up like a drum machine,

wires everywhere. Measuring her
beats. One, one, three, two eventually becomes
one, two, three, four. I don't remember

what it was like when my lungs
arrived under water, already expert
swimmers. More fish than flesh. I just

know what it feels like to be a new
parent. In and out of emotional control,
drowning in panic before everything

finds its steady pulse.

"Sleep When the Baby Sleeps,"

they say.

As if sleeping
is a switch
easily turned on.

Especially when
all of your
mind's power
is being used
for the electricity
of fatherhood.

Especially when
you know that
a dad could be a God,
but you are
a feminist.

Especially when
your daughter's breathing
could brush the quiet
off of a cloud,

but you
keep checking
for storms
through
weather-worn
insomnia.

What if
a baby
is a poem?

Ask me to sleep
through *that*.

Where every breath
is a mirror fog
writing itself
through unstable,
forgetful darkness
and each mind twitch
is a pen stroke.

No matter
what happens,

the words
will be written,
a mouth
will be fed,
a woman
will be born,
a person
will be an echo

and your eyelids
will be heavy
with daylight.

The Sequel

The flesh
stretches
with age,
muscle,
and bone
until it
learns
its parameters.

The rulebook
of nature
can have
many chapters,
but there
is always
an ending -

always
the author's
last word,
typed out
on recycled paper
that's easily
torn,
soul ripped
from storyline.

But the mind
is not
a prisoner
of time.

Imagination
invented the book,
and the brain
made the paper.

A good story
can last
for generations
and inspire
new narratives,
even better
than the last,

more powerful
than any
pre-planned
plot twist,

rewriting
and reinventing itself
until your history
is reborn.

Skin to Skin

Learn how   to   do things
                with one   hand:
           Make a   cheese omelet,
     rescue the   sacrificial
pacifier   from   floor dust,
        answer   the   client's   email,
    pour   orange juice   in   a   glass
                 and add champagne,
cover   your child's   ear
       and   take   note
of   everything
   that   claims   its own   volume,
       bend   down   on   one   knee
                to feed the cat,
                    type   this   poem,
write   the   setlist
                   for   the   show,
       flex your   dad   muscle,
                    dance and sway
to   Brittany Howard's   new album,
fix the record
if a   track   skips.

          Do all of   this
                    as   baby   sleeps
       in   your   other   arm,
round face
       pressed   against   chest,

deep rhythm
breath.

Still Life

Love is
a punctual
stranger,
asking for
change
while I
spend
money
and
time
on broken
clocks,
always
late.

The Birth of All Things

The heartbeat miracle. Cadence of creation. 150 beats
per minute of pure God sound. A tiny thing,
constantly growing. Music of the body. Energy in form.

The birth of all things.

The shadow self. The father's joy. The dad's anxiety.
The tightening of the teeth. Mortality as reality. A baby
who will be greater than the parents' ego. The body as
home.

The birth of all things.

The first breath's expression. Light through lungs.
The mother's magnificence. The jealous cat. A quiet
moment's awareness that will transform into
full-mouthed vibration. The prequel as romance.
The sequel: Legacy. The supernatural power of a
woman's frame.

The birth of all things.

The Sorcerer and the Source

Somehow
we found
enough order
and magic
to conjure you
in a world
obsessed with
its chaos.

Somehow
we sparked
so much alchemy
that you appeared
before us
fully formed,
a wizard
of your own making,
a skin-wrapped spirit.

Somehow
women are
the constant makers
of these miracles,

spellbound creators
of mystic
power.

Synesthesia

When you are a baby,
you will fall asleep
to my voice
sounding out
the colors
that came
into my heart's space
from the
vivid surge of emotion
that blanketed our home
since your birth.

I will tuck you
in a wave
of brushstrokes
and watch as you
learn to eventually
invent your own hue:
All singular flare,
and brilliant expression.

When you are an adult,
you will speak
shade and spectrum
with a transparent tongue.

Woman as masterpiece.

Communicating to
a black and white world
in spectral lingo,
and fluorescent dialect.

It will be
our little secret.

High Definition /
The Silvering

Looking
at you
is like
looking
into
a mirror
that has
yet to
be cracked.

You see
yourself
clearly.

No words
for the
light
or the
off-white
glow
you will
be judged for.

No need
to clean
the smudge,
check for vanity,
or constantly
wonder
what's in the
rearview.

Multiplication Process

The moment
of our first kiss,
an adrenaline rush
grew
inside of me.

Up from
the dusted floor
our shoes shuffled in to,
a bar whose voice
was a steady
growth
of volume
and smoke
through liquid conversation.

Your arms
impulsively
and naturally
wrapped themselves
around my waist
while love
grew
within.

From that moment,
it was a skin-touch
to the sky,
a stone
skipping across
the possibility's ocean,

a record
that didn't skip
across sound waves
fading into
the night.

We matured
as our relationship
grew
from lightning fast
moments and
midnight memories
to the gradual
growth
of mornings
breathing next to
each other's nightmares.

Soon, I woke up and
grew
into the idea
of marriage
to solidify
our staying
and the
growth
of a once
unbelievable dream.

From the day
you told me

you were pregnant,
I've watched you
grow
into an instinct
of nature,
a mother and wife
whose life
is now a natural,
organic knowing. You
grew
our daughter
inside of you,
and I
grew
into a father
as our
stable footing
continues to
shift, learn, and
grow ...

On the 120th Day

Her eyes
burn a bright
elaborate shade
of pearl hazel.
And when she cries,
my dark brown soul
is in animation.

Reflector

When will I stop
seeing tired eyes
after waking up
next to mirrors?

Why do I call
the cracks on my face
fault lines?

How does the earth
hold so much weight;
so much anxiousness?

When will I stop
messing with my hair?

When will I break free
from vanity's repetition:

Look for natural light. Don't sit with shadows.
Suck in your stomach when someone takes a full-bodied
picture. Excessive mirrors. Purchase an outfit,
return the outfit after trying it on at home. Selfies on
the way to the poetry show. Selfies in the car. Adjust
brightness. Convince yourself you looked better when
you were a kid. Post that photo on social media.
Obsessively check for likes. Wipe the grease from your
huge forehead. Wipe the shine from your nose. Wipe the
photo from your mind. Take another, take another, take
another ...

How will I not want
to take a photo
of my daughter every day?

How will I not
see perfection
in her complexion
and smooth brown skin tone?

What if someone
says she looks like me?

How will she not be beautiful?

How did I learn
to be okay with
toxic thought?

How do I not
get angry
if someone looks at her
the way I sometimes
look at myself?

BLACK IS THE NEW BLACK

Black music
is greater than
⎵ or equal to the blues.
It's BESSIE SMITH
as empress of analog emotion.
BB KING'S personified guitar string,
BIG MAMA THORNTON'S
"HOUND DOG" voice divine
and bourbon foot stomp...

Black music
is hip-hop.
The pre-digital sound cloud
that takes us high and rising.
Record break spin
with juice and gin,
Native tongue lingo and trap
It's RAPSODY, 808 boom bap,
all beats, high hats and handclaps.
Streams of BLACK THOUGHT
and bass-heavy flow,

Black music is the banjo.
A lost history
untold by radio,
sold from West Africa
to the minstrel show.
It's frying pans and animal skin,
pig ankle strut and jug stomp.
The echoes of UNCLE JOHN SCRUGGS'
claw hammer roots
as RHIANNON GIDDENS
and DOM FLEMONS
retell the truth and hold the flag.

Black music is jazz.
ALICE COLTRANE and her hands
                plucking sound,
   MAX ROACH and his feet
              to the ground,
up and down between dust kick and
                          Snare

JEFF PARKER and the Chicago skyline
pushing the limit of improvisation,
Sample and soul,

Black music is rock and roll.
It's BIG JOANIE and rrriot vibration,
FISHBONE feedback in
full LIVING COLOUR,
the music of a people,
the pulse of its heart,
a house that was built
by SISTER ROSETTA THARPE.

Side 2

Memory Coordinates

Skeletal Remains

Charleston,
what does it feel like
to walk on bones
buried under cobblestones,
historical markers
of muted melanin
with unmarked stories
never told?

The United States of Anxiety

Welcome to the
United States of Addiction.

In this country,
your smart phone
holds more meaningful moments
than your memory.

Here, social media
is social justice
and history is a hashtag
for broken screens
to get their fix.

Here, fame doesn't
lead to fortune –
just first-world problems.

Echo chambers
for people
at war with themselves.

In the United States of Addiction,
the declaration of independence
isn't for independent people –
the quiet-minded
who mind their own business.

In this country,
you can be an activist
by just being active on your phone,
retweeting revolutionary wars,
thumbprints of repetition,
standing up for something
without getting up from your couch,
self-indulgent shouts
with a global view,
but boomerangs of wisdom
from a bedroom in your house.

(This is a patriotic poem.)

Welcome to the
United States of Anxiety.

In this country,
society tell us
our credit should be straight
while selling us
the crooked path
of commercialism.

Here, citizens take CBD oil
between awkward conversation
and the constant chatter of the mind.
Boredom is not an option,
silence is not sustainable.

In the United States of Anxiety,
Instagram spoons with insomnia.

We swipe up and get out of bed,
wide awake with sleepy minds
then daydream of FOMO and flat screens –
the American dream.

(This is a patriotic poem.)

Welcome to the
United States of Assumptions.

In this country,
the color of your skin
allows automatic privilege!

Land, money, power, health,
monuments, legacy, generational wealth ...

Here, anything unfamiliar is dangerous,
anyone who disagrees with you
is the devil.

In the United States of Assumptions,
any poet who speaks about injustice
is an Obama-loving,
hip-hop bumping,
tree hugging,
emotional heartbeat pumping
soul of a man.

(On the surface,
that may be true about me
but there's many more layers
for you to see ...)

Welcome to
the United States of Aggression.

In this country,
we freely walk over broken bones
in the basement of buildings
built by the kidnapped and enslaved.

Here, we walk on beautiful landscapes
and dance on graves.

Welcome to America,
a walking contradiction.

This is a patriotic poem.

BLACK NUMEROLOGY
(for Walter Scott)

Walter Scott,
I've watched
your death
hundreds of times.
Recently,
I counted
the steps
it took
before the eighth shot
grounded you:
13.

You took
13 paces,
running for
your life,
in line and
online,
the warrior stride
of a 50-year-old
body
that died
too soon.

I wonder
how many
impressions
your feet made
before that
moment.

You probably
walked
hundreds of miles
alive
prior to
poets putting
numbers
on your death march,
countless footsteps
covering the earth
as a son,
a forklift operator,
massage therapist,
father of four.

I wonder
how many
more miles
you would have
walked
holding your
grandchildren.
Would they
have been aware
of the
deep layers
of dark blues
you carried
as a black man
living in the South?

My mouth
is tired of
sounding out the syllables
it takes to talk
about America's
favorite pastime:
Counting bullets
and burying brown bodies.

The Rain

When the reality
of racism returns,
all joy treads water
in oceans of buried
emotion.

Charleston
is doing
everything it can
to only swim
in a colorless liquid
of calm sea
and blind faith.

But the Lowcountry
is a terrain
of ancient tears,
suffocating through
floods of
segregation.

When gunshots
made waves,
we closed our eyes,
held our breath
and went under.

And we are still
trying not to
taste the salt
of our surrounding blues
or face the rising tide
of black pain.

COPY/PASTE

I.
I have always been the thing
that's not like the other:

The analogue touch
through digital screens,

the bougie drink
at a neighborhood dive,

the black ink
bringing anxious poems
to a comfortable
white sheet of paper.

So it would make sense
to be the only brown body
shopping on busy streets,

walking past
peach-skinned mannequins
that wear rainbow-colored threads,

staring out
from store-front windows,
stuck to each other
in a copy and paste culture,
void of color.

II.
When was the last time
a mannequin had an expressive face
behind the mask?

Behind the blank
glossy-eyed barrier
of a window glass?

When was the last time
you saw a black man
stand strong and unashamed
with his dark, holy features,
center-framed in a bleached-out world,

fully aware of being
the blurred-out version
of his true self?

III.
I am a free token
for closed minds
who are broke with blind eyes, a splash,
a cool glass
for the sun's predictable clash
with Charleston streets.

I am the man
without a mirror,
unable to look at himself
in a place
surrounded by the water's reflection.

Someone who is always seen as the "other"
in a copy and paste culture,
void of color.

IV.
I'm looking for memory coordinates
instead of road maps through familiar places,

I'm looking to unravel headphone cords
in a wireless world,

I'm looking for flesh-colored bandaids
that match my skin tone.

I'm looking
to not be so alone.

Earth Tone

When Maya Angelou was eight years old,
she realized she was superhuman.
Her voice, in earth tone and full power,
caused the death of a monster.

Because of that, she held
her weapon of inflection
inside the body. Unconsciously
sharpening it for five years

until unleashing knightly,
majestic poems through lion-hearted
heat of sound and influence. There's nothing

more brave than being a poet. To
break the lid off of silence, risk
ego death, and know your breath
could change the world.

Hope Is in the Listening

City as sorcerer and storyteller, sharp-eyed
observant, holy grandmother. She's survived 350 years

because the longevity of the Lowcountry requires
a special kind of magic. Today, we are witnesses

to that witchcraft. Citizens of its charm. Today,
she is the voice connecting her family: The tourist

and tour guide, cradling history in their arms
like a crying infant. The LGBTQ+ community,

joyous and resilient in the shadow of hate crimes.
Plantation workers sending one-way postcards

to ghosts. Black poets, the great interpreters
of Southern truth. The farmer, hand delivering

homegrown sunshine. The mayor, whose job is to
see hope through floods and watered-down politics.

Charleston's story should be defined by
this diversity. The sounds of promise and protest.

She may be old, but her best days are ahead.
Whatever challenges await, we will face them together

because she hears us, people of change.
She hears us.

Ambient Noise

At sunrise,
street sweepers
silence the ringing filth
of a late night's vibrato. In

the sneaky hours of the morning,
empty bottles and parking spaces
form a hushed choir, a
privileged quiet, a soundtrack

to the aftermath of the discord
that comes with alcohol. Before noon,

the homeless are a cappella,
writing songs and signs
that read,

"All I want is a joyful duet.
A movement instead of an elegy."

At sunset,
pandemonium presses play
and the chaos loops again.

And They Say the Opposite of Love Is Fear

Something
about
the name
itself
speaks of
symmetry,
duality,
and repetition:

Emmett
Till.

Two E's,
two M's,
and two T's
in the
first name,

two L's
in the
last.

He,
lynched
in the year
of two 5's
in

M-i-
s-s-
i-
s-s-
i-
p-p-
i.

Black poets
have
two things
to write about:

Love
and
this.

The fear
that we
can be
nothing more
than what
happens

over
and
over
again.

The America I Know Could Use a Good Cry

I met America at a neighborhood bar.

He offered me a shot of rum and I reminded him
that Captain Morgan was a slave owner,
so the bartender awkwardly slipped another
liquid lie down my throat. I ordered another
drink and was channeled by dark spirits. The
courage of black ghosts who haunt American
dreams.

I told him I loved him and I wanted him to sleep
well. "But I know I've been in your nightmares,"
I said. "I want to be your friend, but only if it's a
deep relationship. Only if you show me that you
are not scared of your baggage. Bring your whole
history to the table."

America cracked open another beer as a tear ran
down his face. He said,

"I was born in a house not my own, and my
fathers demanded that their portraits
hang on every wall. White paint covers each
brown brick and our backyard is a museum
of unmarked graves."

"Despite this, a garden grows," I said.
"And every home can be torn down
and rebuilt again."

"But I've been told I shouldn't completely let you
in," he said. "Some people in my family stand in
the doorway, blocking the entrance."

He left before I could tell him that my people have a history of finding ways inside broken spaces and making them whole again.

Retelling and
the Remembering

Black spirits can not be absent
from anything. Especially in South Carolina,

where every open, abandoned space
holds a family's erased echo,

and racism is embedded in every memory.
We, the living, have the privilege of being

restful ghosts. We haunt material things,
and hold our history in excess. But here,

and everywhere around us, we walk among
the haunted. An old house can not be entered

without touching its nostalgia. An untold story
is an unmarked grave waiting for revision.

This is why we preserve what was once
condemned: To put fresh ink on faded text

and to remember that we can't erase each other.

Frances
& Betty
& Cicely
& the Others

As if the ability to blow into a horn is more important than the ego balloon it took to suck the air out of a woman's voice. As if *Sketches of Spain* is anything but a masterpiece. As if calling yourself "the prince of darkness" is something to be proud of. As if any moonlight could compete with the power light on my CD player the first time I truly understood jazz illumination. As if the only hits some women will remember you by are the ones that were fist print to skin. As if any rock band could compete with the balls of *Bitches Brew*. As if we are all enablers of dark behavior by not replacing "genius" with "narcissist." As if you weren't a fighter who boxed his way through life and landed every punch. As if you didn't make an impact on every genre in my record collection. As if you never really knew what love was, man.

The Language
We Learn

I.
Masculinity
doesn't have
to be toxic,
but some men
choose to put
poison
on their
tongue.

Foaming
at the mouth
before flinging
unholy thoughts
into action.

Hungry for prey,
licking their lips
as biting words
draw blood.

Women do nothing
to feed
this venom.

Porn and
pop culture
evolved
from paper cuts
to pixels

as men
learned
negative language
and spread it around
like a virus.

II.
The first time
I put poison
on my tongue,
I did not
notice
the taste.

The shared language
of youth
stuck
to the roof
of my mouth.

It was the
bad breath
of boys around me,
leaving an
aroma of adolescence,
ignoring the lessons
of our mothers.

III.
The men
that I know
are repulsed
by the taste
of poison.

We are hungry
for clarification
over contamination,

adjectives
that no longer
melt from objects
to people.

Simply put,
we've freed
ourselves
from the pollution
of the mind.

But,
to all of the women
who have been sexualized,
we apologize.

to all of the women
I have sexualized,

I
apologize.

Test Flight

Black woman's legacy still airborne

or stillborn

waiting for proper flight

or landing

or Netflix special

to lift and tell the story

of a wind walker

or wing walker

we should be looking up to.

I'm still looking up for you, Bessie Coleman

to learn about the true attitude

or the true altitude

it took to smile so big in that 1923 photo,

or walk your way to the final flight.

No landing gear

or press

to properly keep your legend rising

like Amelia

or Orville

or Wilbur.

A Divine Feminine

If you believe
superheroes didn't exist,
then you never knew
Georgia Mae Jones.

My grandmother.

She could have
saved the world
with her poundcake.
It had just the right amount of sugar
to defeat any evil
inside of you,

and could
turn a sour weakness
into sweetness,
take your tastebuds
to hyperspace,
and awaken the superpowers
of your senses.

Her heroic hands
held secrets.
Magic spells
mixed into recipes.
An infusion of soul.

The miracle
of a black woman's
kitchen.

Food was one
of her many
strengths,
and it was the one thing
that always brought
my family together.

My life's story
was a gift
through experience,
a moveable feast of memory
that followed me
from childhood to adulthood,
influencing the way
I now interact with flavor,
defining my
standard
of perfection.

I invite you
to rediscover your
story:
To re-read
the ingredients
of your life written by
the supernatural wisdom
of women.

Maybe it's
a divine feminine
that flows through you,
a spellbinding strength

embedded in
your breath,

maybe it's a matriarch's
recipe passing through generations
as you pass through
life.

Or maybe
it's the awareness
that your story
is our story,

and we are permanently
connected
by this
consciousness.

Call Me

by my truth
before you
call me
by my name.

And if you
don't know
my name,
I'd rather
you make up
something Black,
like "Tyrone"
or "Malcolm"
or, better yet,
"King."

And if you
ever hear
my name,
know that it
does not,
in any way,
sound like
the slur
that came
out of
your filthy
mouth.

Movement's Mother

I.
There are spirits
among us.
Ghosts of grassroots movements
echoing through our soil.

Charleston's poinsettia
was a warrior woman
who blossomed
despite an unholy city's
unsettled winds.

She was light
through dark matter,
a sunflower
through storms,
a teacher
of feminism and freedom
with lessons
overstepping limitations
for a nation
that needed to move forward.

Stillness
was not an option.

II.
There's a song among us.
An out-of-tune harmony
written by deep-rooted pain
with racism's wretched refrain.

But,
a daughter of the Lowcountry
became the conductor
of change:
Clearing the air
for a chorus
of beautiful black voices.

Because silence
was not an option.

III.
There's still worry within us.
Tireless activists have died
running marathons
with worn-out tears,
weary with fear,
blinded by lies.

But we can look
through the visionary eyes
of Septima P. Clark.

She,
who taught giants
how to be tall.

She,
who humbly rose so high
that heavenly elevation
is normalized.

Falling down
is no longer an option.

A BRIEF SUMMARY of WHAT THE POET CAN DO
(the spark, part 2)

The poet
uses the
electricity
of a stage
to wire in
to their higher self
with a voice
and a microphone chord
vibrating through floorboards,
sending lyrical lightning bolts
that set
eardrums afire.
LISTEN! Pause and pay attention.
If you do,
a poet's words
can ignite the mind,
throw ash on already

hot emotion,
set memory
to burn,

bring to ~~e~~ smolder
what simmers
beneath skin,
make heat
where the cold
has settled in.

If the listener's mind
is singed,
they'll finger snap —
which carries
as much ~~impact~~ impact
as a handclap.

Poetic energy
traveling through body,
thumbs pressed
against finger
for love recognition
and spoken word
        tradition.

For a musician,
that's a foot tap
or a palm
patting beats
on a knee cap
when a song
unwraps
from your brain
to your ears
to your lungs
to your lap.

But poets
gather around
speech
like bonfire.

Each spark
making contact.

Side 3

Flow Own Current

Antenna

Cover my skin in sorrow.
Lay my body down
with feathered tears.
Help me sleep
with the dreams
of friends who are
having conversations
with ghosts
so that I can wake
with their pain.
A shared depression,
a thread among empaths.
Give me the compassion
and emotional power
to be strong
when needed.

When Falling Into Fear Is Easier Than Falling Asleep

My cat doesn't like car rides.

An otherwise fierce feline
becomes a furry bundle
of fear. Rapid-fire breathing
and foaming at the mouth.

Every second is suffocation,
every bump in the road
is permission
for each hard breath
to be a puke premonition:
On my feet,
my lap,
the back seat.

But she paws her way
through the experience
if only to see the other side:
The calm of a comfort zone
for a creature of habit.
Couch napping, relaxing
quietly, at home.

I am also a habit creature.

Calm in certain places.
Crazy in others.

My claws rarely clutch
unscratched surfaces.
My ears cling
to the silence between
unfamiliar sounds.

Sometimes my days
are spent
doing the same things
over and over
and over
and over again
that the cycle doesn't seem like a circle,
and I've convinced myself
that the s**t in my litter box
doesn't smell so bad.

I've grown into a lion,
but I act like a kitten.

Free me from
the fact that sometimes
I can't see my power.

Free me from the need
to be perfect.

To only reveal
the wings that don't
shed feathers
when I fly through storms.

Free me from the phobia
of showing you *my* fear.

The People's Pandemic

I've been talking about the end of the world
with everyone. Until now, we did everything
we could to not think about death or the
moments meant for stress muscle. But fear is
sustenance, and we now hold solitude tighter
than meat on the bone. Plus, there's some
sort of invisible unease taking over, and we
are all looking for the vaccine to the virus.
The common life cure. I remind people that
this kind of sickness can not compare to the
malady of the mind. But I'm unsure if I
believe it. For now, I'm thankful for the
conversations I'm having. Like this one, with
the restaurant owner, who handed me a bag
of pancakes, an egg sandwich and two
mimosas in a paper bag. With gloves on.
*"How are you handling this mess? The end
of the world." "It's pretty nuts, but I'm
doing the best I can."* Or this one, with the
person in the empty co-working space: *"How
are you handling this mess? The end of the
world." "I'm trying not to look at the news,
because it makes me anxious."* That's it.
Little exchanges. Just enough to affirm the
human. We will make each other proud one
day to say we survived this. But I'm unsure if
I believe it.

20 'til Infinity

look   at   us!
footsteps   making   echo   sound
on   sidewalks.
black   men   leaning   in   for   a   head   nod
instead   of   a   handshake.
loneliness   as   survival.
curbside   cocktails.
men   in   masks
walking   pit   bulls.
parents   loving
and   loathing
school   shutdowns.
cigarette   smoke   dancing
around   silent   porch
g   a   t   h   e   r   i   n   g   s   .
physical   and   emotional
distance.   paranoia,
as   in
"can   the   trees   spread   disease?"
ghost   streets.
some   of   us
taking   slow   breath
in   the   middle   of
fast   ration.
dark   mode   option
of   the   internet.
moms   with   strollers,
coffee   and   cellular   phones.
bicyclists   letting   us   in
on   the   mid   day   sun   secret.
still   finding   time   to
put   on   lipstick.

80

mind   and   body   going   in   circles,
off   balance.
prayers   up
through   pollution.
janet   jackson
in   headphones
sampling   joni   mitchell's
big,   truth   chorus.
this   is   how   we   chill
from   2020   'til.

How to Get Published

Contemporary:
Speak of bone
And elegy.
Obscure reference.
Bat Face Cuphea.
Take out the plural.
Submit for a chance
To talk in circles.
Find the press
And make poetry
Your business.
Intimacy of page.
Example ...

Spoken word:
Speak black tongue
until you spit black.
Overshare.
Stir the human
with the humor.
Political as personal.
Use figurative language
so much
it comes out of
your mouth
like liquid flower flow.
Example: See above.

Instagram:
Don't speak.
Flowers and text
on white background.
Sage advice.
Burn sage.
The simple
as profound.
Post until it
means something.

— example.

The Colossal

Depression and anxiety,
you are not just
the elephant in the room,

you are
the weight that holds
the animal,

the air shared
with its shadow,

the zoo that
won't release
a caged mind.

Depression and anxiety,
you are not just
the elephant in the room,

you are
the ceiling below
the sky,

the mosquito
flying around
its head,

the dust
and dirt
surrounding
scarred feet,

the dry ivory touch
of bone
beneath skin.

Depression and anxiety,
you *are* the elephant in the room,

but you will not be
bigger than me,

and you will not
be the death
of me.

Let's Talk About
the Weather

Light follows us
wherever we go,
no matter how shadowed
the mind.

But darkness
has a sneaky way
of taking us over
at night,
and sometimes
its sleepy residue
remains in the day

in spite
of the sun's
warm personality
and efficient,
persistent glow.

We sleep
through hot nightmares
when the only cool air
is the pushback
of bedsheets.

When we awaken
to a cold daydream,
we'll shine
through the suffering,

sacrifice ourselves
for small talk
and push our bodies
to the limit,

hoping to be
blessed
by the
Goddess of the sky.

When we talk
about the weather,
let's not be afraid
to speak the truth
about our flooded emotions.

When there are oceans
of ready-made disasters
throwing shade
at the summer,

let's be there
for each other.

Give
shelter.

Dandruff

On a head full of hair,
there will always be weak strands.
Knots on the brain
are also knots in the stomach.
Itch buildup.
Gut-touched
twists too tight
on the scalp.
Don't cut them off
or wish for an unraveling.
Instead,

be thankful that
dry skin can still
wear a crown.
Be aware
of the muscle to burn
when you eventually
brush the dirt
off your shoulders.

Cadence

Time takes itself
too seriously.

Look at the way
it weighs us down
with slow-bent bones,
a romanticism of memory,
a constant discourse
toward death.

Will time ever lighten up?

It can choose to remind us
about the poetic
strokes of life. Like,
silver hair in a golden age
or the growing knowledge
that blooms from experience.

But time
is too moody and scattered.

Forever shifting
from one moment
to the next,
with a carefully-planned cadence,
never standing still.

Dancing to a
deliberate,
downbeat
tempo.

Wordplay (Remix)

Did you know that
poets are superheroes?

We have a God-like grasp
of language
and the power
to transform
any emotion
into alliteration.

We sit with sadness
until it spins
out of silence
on to paper,
we craft
confessional poems
with the spark
of a metaphor
and the speed
of a comet,
we are saviors of sonnets.

Protectors of expression.

If there is no answer,
poets write down
the question.

Did you know that
poets are rappers?

Sometimes we'll rhyme
in standard time
where every other line
is a rhythmic sound,
we'll bring you in
with the stroke of a pen
and make you believe
every word is profound.

Our books are bound
to be mirrors of thought,
transparent voices
for hidden pain.

And spoken word poets
scream so loud
our voices become
melodic refrains.

Did you know that
poets are mathematicians?

We solve puzzles
with wordplay,
using couplets of description.

We obsess over scores
for slam competitions,
we carefully count syllables
when writing haikus,

we painstakingly pick out
six-line patterns for sestinas.

There's palindromes,
pantoums, villanelles,
and prose.

Poems are meticulously
and miraculously
mapped out like calculus.

Did you know that
poets are astronauts?

We can be weightless
with writer's block
or gridlocked
with gravity.

We'll take our words
from the page to the stage
to the planets,
from abstract ideas
to the proof of new galaxies,

where synonyms
become stanzas,
then satellites
of sound.

Side 4

Affirm the Human

On Headphones

Muscle
memory
through
music
releases
sound waves
of remembrance
through
my body.

And I
realize
I am
a little boy
sleeping
in a
man's frame,
sentimental
and sensitive
to the
audible
accents
of melody
ringing
through
my years.

Black Magic, Black Muse (A Poem 4 Prince)

Alone, on your last night alive,
with your voice unamplified,
did you speak in perfect pitch
like you sang, one week prior?
57 and flawless,
fans hanging on every word,
melodies triggering memories,
a Prince with a piano and microphone.

Alone, on your last night alive
did you have the same confidence
you had when you were 19?
Planting the seed
for a global funk garden:

Your left eye on music,
your right eye on sex,
your third eye on Jesus.

Songs pouring out of you
with the mystery of miracles,
verses written like scripture,
each drumbeat
a hypnotic hip-nod to the holy.

Alone, on your last night alive,
did gold fall from the sky
of your studio like rain
as it did when you were 37?

Nasty and nameless,
a "slave" to no one but your muse,
guitar solos spilling out of you
like sorcery,
albums defying the speed of sound.

Were you always aware of your witchcraft
or were you secretly scared of it?

Did you know that your death
would blanket the world
in purple shadow?

Did you know that we would spend
a million days just scratching the surface
of your memory?

Our love, like jazz
is an electric harmony
that now digs through
your digital garden
searching for unity,
starving for melody.

In the blurry confusion of your death,
the world sharpened its focus on the '80s
when people of all colors
had purple skin.

A psychedelic blend
of red and raspberry,
when a lavender legacy of hits
made us party like it was *1999*.

It was a *Sign 'O' the Times.*

As radio changed,
your voice stayed the same.
New lotus flowers grew
from your paisley playground,
the sun, the moon and stars
were at your whim,
you gave us the future of soul in *20Ten*
and *The Rainbow Children*
danced again.

Alone, on your last night alive,
with your voice unamplified,
were you still blessed and possessed
with passion?

Were you writing the greatest song
that we'll never get to hear?

Did you know that you'd disappear?

Were you lonely?

Sleater-Kinney

A vocal explosion

    of too hot energy.

Fluid heat in headphones.

    Smoke, thrashing out of stereo speakers

with each flash of sound,

        while drugged-up

stale, pale, male

    "rock Gods" continue to

      rattle dry bones

with thinly veiled water-down blues,

      Carrie Brownstein infuses

guitar strings with gasoline,

~~Janet Weiss~~

    lights torches on the tops of drums

and Corin Tucker

    is the inferno

      and the fury.

Björk Crawls Into My Ears

Sometimes I put *Utopia* on the coffee table just
to see the reaction. There's Björk, on brand.
Peach round angles and alien stare. Blue hair and
perched lips, eyes cut from cobalt. Vagina
forehead. A flute on purple goo. Behold this
fearlessness! Is she flesh or computer? Since the
late '70s, she's been a God star. Essence of
innovation. Electronic wizard producer and
voice. Yes, that voice. All color and other
planetary. There's nothing like it. Back to *Utopia*:
Don't stop at the album cover. Press play and
ignite all senses. Is that a bird or a button-pushed
sequence? Are you hearing this? A harp in
spacetime with ultra-fine melody. Phantom
undertone bass. Björk, you are an other
dimension of song, and I see you for who you are.

When I'm at Home, I Watch Star Wars. When I Watch Star Wars, I Write Haikus About War, Violence, and Memory.

Episode 1
Battle droid theory:
Turn war into fetish, make
army of robots.

Episode 2
Soldiers are now slaves
in galaxies of mass graves,
programmed for violence.

Episode 3
Fear is mutation,
soul transformation and sin
when man starts to kill.

Episode 4
The family back home:
Echoes and faint memories
of life before war.

Episode 5
Too dark, now. Mind filled
with trauma and torture. Mask
for the suffering.

Episode 6
Confront the demon.
Put end to internal war.
Make peace before death.

Episode 7
A ghost's memory
haunts the new generation
and passes down pain.

Episode 8
Young resistant minds
have the spark to start over.
Reclaim history.

Episode 9
If demon returns,
reprogram memory, and
write your own story.

THE ARRIVAL

Looking up
and back
at the cliff
of regret.
Feet, adjusting
to the lack
of quicksand,
the cleanliness
of solid ground.
Jumping felt good!
Landing feels better.

Heart tells mind,
"Let's do that
again."

About the Author

Marcus Amaker was named Charleston, SC's first poet laureate in 2016.

He's also the award-winning graphic designer of a national music journal (*No Depression*), an accomplished electronic musician, the creator of a poetry festival, and a mentor to hundreds of students.

His poetry was published alongside two national book award winners in an anthology of African American poetry, and has been featured by PBS Newshour, SC Public Radio, Huffington Post, A&E Network, *Charleston Magazine, Charleston City Paper, North Dakota Quarterly, The Post and Courier, Charleston Scene,* and several other publications.

In 2019, he won a Governor's Arts award in South Carolina, and was named the artist-in-residence of the Gaillard Center, a world-renowned performance and education venue.

His poetry has been studied in classrooms across the country, and has been interpreted for ballet, jazz, modern dance, opera and theater.

Marcus has recorded three albums with Grammy Award winning drummer and producer Quentin E. Baxter of Ranky Tanky.

This is his eighth book. Visit him at **marcusamaker.com**

About the Artist

Nick Davis is a digital artist. He is inspired by Kerry James Marshall, Kehinde Wiley, and Kara Walker. He uses his art to express things he can't say. As a person who deals with anxiety and depression, his goal is simply to encourage his community and others that they are not alone and that their Black Is Beautiful. Visit him on Instagram at **instagram.com/ndartlife.**

Acknowledgements and Notes

Early versions of some of these poems appeared in *North Dakota Quarterly, Charleston City Paper,* the film "Mr. Nelson On The North Side" (Kew Media Distribution), *The Electric City News, The Post and Courier,* and online.

"Let's Talk About the Weather" was the first poem written for this collection. "Multiplication Process" is for Jordan Amaker. "Frances & Betty & Cicely & the Others" is about Miles Davis. For a break down of every poem in this book, visit **marcusamaker.com/thebirthofalithings.**